The Naming of Nochebuena in the Midnight Play

Archway Publishing books may be ordered through booksellers or by contacting:

Archway Publishing
1663 Liberty Drive
Bloomington, IN 47403
www.archwaypublishing.com
844-669-3957

Because of the dynamic nature of the Internet, any web addresses or links contained in this book may have changed since publication and may no longer be valid. The views expressed in this work are solely those of the author and do not necessarily reflect the views of the publisher, and the publisher hereby disclaims any responsibility for them.

Interior Image Credit: Moch. Fajar Shobaru

ISBN: 978-1-6657-6909-9 (sc)
978-1-6657-6911-2 (hc)
978-1-6657-6910-5 (e)

Library of Congress Control Number: 2024924701

Print information available on the last page.

Archway Publishing rev. date: 12/13/2024

The Naming of Nochebuena in The Midnight Play

By

Michele Jeanmarie

In a small rural village, there lived a little girl who walked three miles down the mountain, over the bridge, through the village plaza to school every morning, rain or shine. Every day on the way to school she admired the Christmas decorations as they went up. First scantily, and then abundantly, colorful lights cascaded from the village rooftops toward the middle of the plaza. The season of Christ Child's Birth was nearing, and the village buzzed with cheerful greetings and joyful laughter.

As she meandered along the circular cobblestone paved plaza, the little girl glanced at her index cards, muttering to herself. She was memorizing her lines for the play. The teacher had assigned her to portray Mary. The little girl walked by and smiled with everyone, as their paths crossed.

"What must she be doing?" asked a boy, as he helped his father during one last minute addition of a fiery dressed angel to the plaza gate door.

When the little girl saw this, she hopelessly wondered, "How nice would it be if my family had an angel for the church."

"She's studying for a play that'll be given by the church, the night before Christmas. We will all attend and celebrate this special occasion!" explained his father.

The little girl marched on. Although she felt happy, there were, at times, lines that zigzagged her forehead.

All her friends were contributing something toward the church's decorations. She had nothing.

She pondered and pondered, but whenever she came up with something, it was much too costly for her family.

The villagers were beautifully decorating the church. They were polishing all the statues of saints. They were replacing all the burnt candles. They were waxing the altar. They were crowning the Christmas tree, better known as the Advent Tree, for it is the period before the coming of Christ Child. There were gifts for the orphans.

As some parishioners were decorating the church, the cast of the Midnight Play was rehearsing. Young Mary steadily walked toward her group.

"Do you know why we go to mass at midnight," asks a voice, the inner voice of Chela. *"We go at midnight to keep vigil, to keep watch, to wait for an announcement, in this case, the birth of Baby Jesus."*

As she walked, her head lit up with red, green, blue and white lights. Her mind, however, was on the Midnight Play.

Dressed in a royal blue gown and matching *babuchas* on her feet, she was lying on a cot, when the Angel Gabriel appeared in the foreground and said, "You will bear a son, and you shall call his name Jesus."

"But how can that be possible, seeing that I know not a man?" asked Mary.

And the angel said unto her, "the Holy Spirit shall come upon thee."

"I am the handmaid of the Lord," obeyed Mary.

And off the stage walked the Angel Gabriel. Mary then leaped up and hastily walked off the stage.

At the foot of the stage, the chorus sang.

Chela begins to muse, inwardly,

Mary, pregnant with Baby Jesus goes to visit her cousin, Elizabeth, elderly and unable to get pregnant, but is now pregnant with John the Baptist, Jesus' cousin. In Mary's presence, John the Baptist leaps in his mother's womb. Elizabeth announces this, and greets her, "Mary full of grace...," a greeting that is now a prayer for millions of Catholics.

Chela recollects the story of King David. In the presence of the ark, the ark which housed the manna, the tablets, and Aaron's staff, he, King David, had also leaped for joy when the ark had been returned to his house.

See, Chela muses on, when King David was transferring the ark to Jerusalem, it was quite unstable. Someone reached out to stabilize it, but was struck dead, for he was not a priest, he was not allowed to touch the ark. King David grew afraid, so he sent the ark away, to someone else's home. The ark had stayed away for three months. Mary was three months pregnant with Baby Jesus. During these three months, the homeowner had grown rich and wealthy. King David saw this and asked for the ark to be returned to him. Upon its arrival, King David skipped with joy, like John the Baptist, who had skipped with joy in his mother's womb, in the presence of pregnant Mary.

That being, Mary became known as the new ark.

You know what else, "Three, three and three. Very trinitarian. Throw in the mix is Moses, who had also stayed with his mother for three months before he was sent off floating in a basket towards the pharaoh's daughter.

When the chorus paused, a nobleman of Caesar Augustus's empire ran unto the stage, dropped the decree and yelled, "all the world should be taxed."

Passersby scurried along the stage. Joseph also marched into Judea to be taxed with his espoused wife, Mary, being great with child.

As Mary and Joseph tiredly walked the stage, the chorus sang. The chorus paused and so did they. Joseph knocked on a door and asked, "Is there a place for us to rest?"

"We have no room," replied the innkeeper.

Joseph knocked on another door and again asked, "Is there a place for us to rest?"

And, again, the reply was the same. "We have no room."

So, Mary and Joseph proceeded to walk in circles on the stage, while the prop team set up a manger. Joseph led Mary in and helped her unto a cot.

"Manger? Do you know what manger means in French? It means, 'to eat,' and when Baby Jesus grew up and died, he became spiritual food, the bread. This was foreshadowed in the Old Testament, thousands of years before, when it rained down on the Israelites to be eaten as food."

A cry came out.

The chorus began to sing as the shepherds marched unto the stage, tending to the lambs, when an angel of the Lord appeared, "I bring you good news. For unto you is born this day in the city of David a Savior, which is Christ the Lord. And this shall be a sign unto you; ye shall find the babe wrapped in swaddling clothes, lying in a manger."

The chorus and everyone on the stage proclaimed, "Glory to God in the highest, and on earth peace, good will toward men!"

The angel left the stage, and the shepherds said to one another, "Let us now go into Bethlehem, and see this thing which the Lord has made known to us."

They walked in circles until finally they stopped in front of Mary and Joseph and the babe lying in a manger.

The chorus sang while Mary and Joseph walked off the stage. Other shepherds joined the few on the stage. Blocking the manger, the shepherds at a time explained, "Christ the Lord is born!"

"Christ the Lord is born!"

Herod the King appeared on the opposite side of the stage, which he paced with a perplexed look on his face. He summoned the Three Wise Men and said unto them, "Go and search diligently for the young child, and when ye have found him, bring me word, so that I may come and worship him also."

The Wise Men slowly wandered, looking up on occasion at the star in the east placed on a starry black background. On a brief stop, one said, "Where is he that is born King of the Jews? For we have seen his star in the east and have come to worship him."

They finally stopped in front of the manger when Mary and Joseph reappeared.

Chela explains,

Do you know the Three Wise Men were gentiles, non~jews? They were called Gaspar, Melchor and Baltazar. They came to fulfill the promise that Abraham's descendants will be as numerous as the stars. His descendants will include all mankind, and so it is no surprise that non~Jews will be present to welcome the new King, the Messiah.

The magi, as they are also known, presented Baby Jesus with frankincense, gold, and myrrh.

"How odd," might have been a question of both Mary and Joseph. "Why would our baby be given frankincense, gold, and myrrh? First, it was his conception, then threats on his life, now frankincense, gold and myrrh from people not of her clan."

Mind you, these signaled the life Baby Jesus was to lead.

The Old Testament, written a few thousand years earlier, mentioned that a lamb will arrive on the scene, and its legs will not be broken, because he is to expiate all sins. He is to forgive all sins. As it occurred, this lamb would grow up to be no other than Jesus.

Mary and Joseph knew the Torah very well. They were all taught about their faith. Lamb? Savior? Messiah? Me? Us?

Gaspar spoke first, "I bring thee, Christ the Lord, frankincense.

For we are to worship you. As the Son of God, he would be divine. Thinks Chela.

'Christ' is Greek for Savior. How would they know that? Chela asks herself.

Baltazar followed, "I bring thee, Christ the Lord, gold.

For you are Son of God, a deity, a royal, as King of the Jews. Figures Chela.

Melchor ended, "I bring thee, Christ the Lord, myrrh.

For someday, it'll be used to prepare you for burial. Forecasts Chela.

And upon presenting their gifts, the Three Wise Men stood up and paced the stage. An angel appeared and warned, "Do not return to King Herod." And so, the Three Wise Men departed for their own country using an alternative route.

In the manger, the babe, Joseph and Mary slept on the cot when an angel appeared over Joseph and said, "Arise and take the young child and his mother, and flee into Egypt, for Herod will seek to destroy him."

Egypt? That's where Moses was taken from the river. He was raised in Egypt. That's where their people were mistreated. But, obeyed they did, and confidently proceeded to Egypt.

Do you know something else? Do you know that Moses prefigures Jesus, the Lord? Check this out:

Moses delivered his people out of Egypt.
Jesus delivered mankind out of sin.

Moses stayed with his mother to be nursed for three months.

Jesus was three months in his mother's womb when he was presented to his cousin, John the Baptist, who was six months old in his mother's womb.

Moses performed many miracles.
Jesus performed many miracles.

Moses went up Mount Sinai.
Jesus went up the Mount of Transfiguration.

On Mount Sinai, Moses came close to God.
On Mount of Transfiguration, Jesus became God
and, thus, came face to face with Moses and Elijah.

From Mount Sinai, Moses came down
with a face that had been illuminated.
Jesus, too, appeared to his disciple~friends
with a face that shone like the sun, while
his garments were as white as the snow.

Moses was handed the Ten Commandments.
Jesus summed up the Ten Commandments in
one sentence, "Love one another as oneself."

Mind~blowing!

When they heard this, Joseph and Mary, with the babe, arose and hurriedly walked off the stage.

The chorus sang. A member lifted a sign that read, "Herod is dead!"

Joseph, Mary and the young child returned to the stage, to Nazareth. The shepherds and all the angels joined them and in spirit, they all exclaimed: And the grace of God was upon him!

A great big bang shocked the little girl out of her daydream. She found herself sitting on a pew and turned her attention toward the loud noise. Someone else had dropped off a case of food by the Advent Tree.

She was saddened once again, but this time, joined the cast on the stage. She fumbled a lot. She was late in saying her lines. She was too early in saying them. Sometimes, she did not even say them. She was nudged. She was fanned. She was sometimes even ushered. If only a miracle could happen to her on her return to church, as it had to Mary.

She left the church and once again, walked past the plaza, through the village, over the wooden bridge, up the mountain, all the while hoping for a miracle. She drew near her house, but nothing happened.

The next day, she embarked back up the road. Determined not to enter empty-handed, she picked up three spiky green leaves from the side of the road, which she placed in her backpack.

As she was approaching the plaza gate-door, the same young boy, who had been helping his father hang the fiery dressed angel to the door, rushed from behind her and handed her more spiky green leaves. She smiled and thanked him but decided to leave them behind. The little boy persuaded her to take them. Take them, she did.

She got to church and handed the spiky green leaves to a fellow churchgoer, who then placed them into some water on the altar.

Days had gone by. It was now Christmas Eve and time for the rendition of the "Midnight Play." The little girl and her family walked through the church's main door, and in front of her, in the same place where stood the green spiky leaves, were now beautiful, majestic *nochebuenas*.

Nochebuenas, translated verbatim, means good nights.

Nochebuena, in its singular form, means Christmas Eve.

From that day on,
Nochebuenas became the Christmas flower, the poinsettias.

And so, the little girl proudly approached the cast of the Midnight Play, as her parents and her guardian angel, as she now calls him smiled on. She played a brilliant part, executed it magnificently. She beamed with pride and joy. The same insignificant leaves that she contributed to the church, beamed with color and life.

And every day of the year, ever since then, and especially during Christmas, when she sees poinsettias color the hallways and shelves and tables of every store, market or home, she ponders on the miracle of the night before Christmas.

Character Analysis

Thinking of Mary and Joseph fleeing, which other stories or fairy tale come to mind? Compare and contrast them. (The Three Billy Goats Gruff; The Three Little Pigs; The Seven Dwarfs; The Three Bears; The Wizard of Oz; Little Red Riding Hood)

Example:

Title of stories of my choice:	The Midnight Play	Batman
Villain(s)	King Herod	The Joker
Attributes	Mean, powerful	Mean, clever
Mission Objective	To remain in power	Overtake Gotham City
Method	To kill all male babies under the age of 2	Entrapment
Mission Accomplished	No	No
Moral of the Lesson	Humility	Humility

There are many laws and credos against immigration. Research one. Compare and contrast Joseph and Mary's entry to Egypt to any immigrant of your choice in your city.

	Joseph and Mary	Immigrant of your choice
Reason for leaving their country		
Laws of the time		
Reception in host country		
Conclusion		

Joseph took his espoused wife, Mary, to be taxed. When were taxes implemented in your country? Why? What are the benefits of paying taxes? The repercussions? What would have happened to Joseph had he not gone to pay his taxes? What are the repercussions if your parents do not pay their taxes?

	Judea	Your country
When were taxes implemented		
Benefits of paying taxes		
Reception in host country		
Conclusion		

Comprehension

The protagonist does not have a name. What would you name her? Why?

The author mentions an Advent Tree. Do you initiate the season with an Advent Tree? How?

In writing, an easter egg is often a surprise. How was the easter egg inserted in the story? What has the "Easter Egg" revealed?

Writing Convention

The author used a lot of repetition. In the following, circle the repeated word. Then re-write it with as few words as possible.

She fumbled a lot. She was late in saying her lines. She was too early in saying them. Sometimes, she did not even say them. She was nudged. She was fanned. She was sometimes even ushered.

Printed in the United States
by Baker & Taylor Publisher Services